Cryptocurrency

An Exposé On Ensuring Online Safety And Security: The Significance Of Blockchain Technology And Comprehending Digital Currency

(A Comprehensive Handbook On Cryptocurrency Trading And Investment)

Kendrick Villanueva

TABLE OF CONTENT

Introduction 1

Utilizing Chart Patterns For Discerning Bearish And Bullish Market Trends! 4

The Prospects And Potential Of Cryptocurrency In The Future 22

Acquisition Methods For Cryptocurrencies 25

Comparing Day Trading With Long-Term Investing 30

Blockchain..74

Introduction 98

Computation And The State Of Being Turing-Complete... 111

Cryptocurrencies Often Fail... 124

The Prevalent Currencies In The Global Foreign Exchange Market... 135

Introduction

Initially, Allow Me To Elucidate The Manner In Which You Can Effectively Leverage The Bitcoin Derivatives Market To Your Advantage. In Relation To Conducting A Comprehensive Analysis, As Well As When Endeavoring To Ascertain The Future Trajectory Of Bitcoin's Value In Order To Provide You With The Necessary Tools To Gain A Competitive Advantage In The Market. Subsequently, I Will Present To You The Distinctiveness Associated With Conducting Independent Research On Digital Currencies. I Will Also Disclose The Research Methodology I Personally Employ, As Thorough Analysis Will Aid You In Determining Which Cryptocurrencies To Procure And Which Ones To Refrain From. In Addition, Conducting Thorough Research On Cryptographic Currencies Will Facilitate The Identification Of Optimal Buying And Selling Opportunities For These Digital Assets. Henceforth, I Shall Provide You With My Foremost

Projections For Digital Currencies In The Year 2021, Elucidating The Rationale Behind My Predictions, Thereby Allowing You To Comprehend The Forthcoming Trends Within The Crypto Market. Subsequently, I Will Conduct A Comprehensive Analysis Of The Financial Performance Of Diem In Order To Determine The Viability Of Investment. Henceforth, We Shall Delve Into An Esteemed Cryptocurrency Venture Positioned As The Front-Runner Within The Realm Of Decentralized Video Streaming. Furthermore, I Will Provide You With Comprehensive Information Regarding Investing In Smart Contract Cryptocurrencies And The Potential Paradigm Shift This Industry Might Bring To The Realm Of Digital Currencies For Eternity. Henceforth, I Shall Proceed To Elucidate The Methods By Which One Can Invest In Privacy Based Blockchains, Thereby Unlocking The Full Potential Of The Bitcoin Blockchain. Continuing Further, I Will Elucidate The Process Of Investing In Supply Chain Blockchains Such As

Vechain, Waltonchain, And Hedera Hashgraph, As Well As Expound Upon Investing In Stablecoins Such As Usdt, Usdc, And Stellar. Lastly, I Will Elucidate On The Methods For Avoiding Crypto Scams, In Addition To Providing You With A Comprehensive Compilation Of Those That Necessitate Your Vigilance. I Will Also Provide You With Valuable Advice To Prevent Falling Victim To Scams, Fraudulent Techniques, And Unethical Practices.

Utilizing Chart Patterns For Discerning Bearish And Bullish Market Trends!

Price patterns emerge as a result of traders engaging in buying and selling activities at specific levels. Consequently, the price fluctuates within these levels, thereby giving rise to the formation of chart patterns. When the price ultimately exceeds the boundaries of the price pattern, it may signify a substantial shift in sentiment.

Patterns that manifest over an extended duration generally possess greater dependability, giving rise to a singular occurrence of price deviation from the pattern. Similar to the pattern observed on the one-minute chart, the daily chart also exhibits a more substantial magnitude of movement compared to the intra-day chart.

Ascending triangle

Definition: A horizontal alignment is created at the uppermost point through the arrangement of two or more heights that are equal. A horizontal line is intersected by a series of ascending trenches, two or more of which collectively comprise a climbing formation. It typically transpires amidst an upward trajectory.

Regarding commerce: In general, an occurrence of a breakout in alignment with the prevailing trend can be anticipated. The majority of traders are inclined to establish a position once there is a clear breakout above the upper boundary of the triangle pattern, accompanied by a noticeable surge in trading volume. As a result of this breakout, it can be expected that the price will subsequently rise by a magnitude equivalent to the widest segment of the triangle.

Descending triangle

Description: The presence of two or more identical inclines results in the creation of a level, horizontal line at the lower end. Additionally, the occurrence of two or more declining peaks gives rise to a descending line that intersects with the aforementioned horizontal line. It typically assumes a descending pattern.

Commerce: Broadly speaking, there will be a significant movement aligned with the prevailing trend. After the price action experiences a pause as a result of an upsurge in volume at the lower trend line of the triangle, a significant number of traders will initiate trades, leading to a subsequent decrease in price by an amount equivalent to the widest section of the triangle.

Symmetrical triangle

Summary: Symmetrical triangles are formations that occur in financial markets when there is a lack of a definitive trend, signaling a state of ongoing stability. During this period, the peaks and troughs of the data converge at the minimum amplitude that corresponds to the lowermost point of the triangle. This predicament presents a formidable challenge for investors who are tasked with determining the optimal course of action. As investors ascertain their position, it transitions from left to right with a heightened volume compared to the preceding volume prior to the market breakout.

It would be advisable to contemplate initiating trades at breakout points, as this will sustain the long-term trend that has been observed.

Head and shoulders

Summary: This phenomenon can be characterized by the presence of three sequential peaks, with the central peak exhibiting the highest elevation, while the outer two peaks possess lower heights that are relatively similar. It exhibits an ascending trajectory and frequently undergoes a reversal, transitioning from rapid growth to a bearish stance. One of the most reliable trend reversal patterns considered among traders is the head and shoulder pattern.

You will be obliged to exhibit patience until the pattern attains completion and the price breaches beneath the designated threshold subsequent to the culmination of the right shoulder. The predominant point of entry occurs during a breakout, wherein the support line is breached and the decision is made to execute a SELL trade.

The pattern known as "inverted head and shoulders"

Description: The arrangement comprises three consecutive peaks, with the middle peak being the lowest and the two outer peaks having comparable heights. It demonstrates a descending trajectory and frequently indicates a transition from a bearish to a bullish trend.

Trading Strategy: Exercise patience until the pattern fully matures and the price successfully exceeds the established threshold. The prevalent point of entry occurs when there is a breach - the solid line is breached, subsequently leading to the execution of buying and trading activities.

Decrease Channel and Increase Channel

Definition: The demarcation of commerce within two diagonal parallel boundaries. It transpires when there is an upward or downward trajectory observed within the confines of parallel support and resistance boundaries. This implies a potential shift in pattern or an alteration in the trajectory of the existing pattern.

Trading: 1) Upon observing emerging patterns, traders who hold the belief that the price will remain confined within its predetermined range can commence trading once the price exhibits fluctuations within the boundaries of its trend lines, 2) Alternatively, traders can initiate trading when the price surpasses its established pattern, commonly known as a breakout. By analyzing the directional patterns of the channel, whether they ascend or descend. In the case of such an occurrence, there exists the possibility that the price shall exhibit swift movement in the direction of this breakout.

Crimson and downward-pointing banners

Description: Brief temporal span (limited period) Compact rectangular commercial demarcation situated amid diagonal parallels. This stands in opposition to the prevailing price trend depicted on the long-term price chart. It primarily manifests following a rapid advancement or decline, indicating a probable shift in direction that precedes the restoration of the previous trend.

Flag patterns can manifest themselves as either an ascent in the market (known as a blush flag) or a descent in the market (referred to as a downward flag). The flag pattern is widely regarded as being among the most dependable continuity patterns employed by traders, as it establishes a strategic opportunity to participate in the ongoing trend that is poised to persist.

Trading: Initiating a trade occurs at the breakout point, provided it aligns with the prevailing market trend. Furthermore, given the presence of swifter flag patterns, traders have a preference for a breakout characterized by heightened trading volume; however, it is important to note that this requirement is unnecessary. The breakout volume must align with the previous volume when considering the bearish flag pattern.

Falling pitcher

Summary: Two contiguous lines are curved in a downward direction. This occurrence commonly takes place subsequent to a period of decline, indicating the potential for a swift reversal of the underlying downtrend. It may appear to indicate an upward trajectory and suggest the possibility of a sustained continuation of a specific trend. In any case, the decline in wages typically leads to a rapid occurrence. The downward movement of a pitcher is a more dependable indicator in contrast to the upward movement of a pitcher.

Exchange: In the event that the price breaches the upper trend line, it is anticipated that the price will ascend. The newly developed patterns can be exchanged among traders who engage in interchanging activities within the convergence lines... Nevertheless, the majority of traders are required to exercise patience until the complete pattern emerges, along with a breakout, following which they may proceed to execute a purchase order.

Rising Wage

The illustration depicts the inclination of two intersecting lines in an upward direction. It typically manifests subsequent to an upward trend, albeit it can also manifest amidst a downward trend. Typically, there is a decline in volume as a result of an increase in price, which occurs within the framework of the pattern known as price/volume deviation. An escalation in pitching typically leads to a state of deterioration.

Trade Opportunities: Convergence lines present potential trading possibilities for swing traders by capitalizing on emerging patterns before breakouts occur. Nevertheless, it would be advised for the majority of merchants to exercise patience and await the complete pattern, including its errors, before proceeding to place a short sale order.

Double down

Description: Two successive, approximately equivalent declines followed by a central apex (resembling a "W" pattern). This chart pattern exhibits a prolonged decline and mainly signifies a reversal pattern suggestive of a temporary deviation from the upward trend. from the downward trend. The expansion in magnitude frequently takes place during the upward price movement within the pattern. The presence of these significant upward spikes in volume strongly suggests an increase in price pressure and serves to affirm the successful occurrence of a double-down pattern.

Trade Opportunity: Once the price breaches the resistance line (also known as the neckline) and successfully forms the pattern, proceed to execute a buy order.

Double top

Explanation: This graphical representation showcases two

consecutive peaks, with a trough in the middle, creating a distinct "M" shape. This chart pattern signifies a temporary deviation from a positive trajectory to a negative trajectory.

Trading Strategy: Once the price surpasses the support line and fully executes the pattern, initiate a short position by placing a sell order.

Triple Bottom

Summary: This comprises a series of three consecutive, nearly identical declines that closely resemble the initial occurrence of a double bottom pattern. These cascades symbolize an unsuccessful endeavor to breach the zone of support. A decline in volume typically accompanies each examination of support, unless there is a price breakout accompanied by heightened volume. This particular trend exhibits a prolonged declining trajectory and frequently serves as an indicator of a reversal pattern signifying a modest, if not protracted, shift in the upward trend (i.e., ascending) from the preceding downward trend.

Trade: Upon the occurrence of the price surpassing the barrier line and successfully finalizing the pattern, execute a purchase order.

Triple top

Description: A series of three consecutive peaks, nearly identical in size, exhibiting similarities to a double top formation upon initial observation. These crests provide an opportunity to observe the endeavors that were unsuccessful in breaching the zone of resistance. Provided that a surge in volume does not result in a price breakout, a decline in volume is observed during the resistance test. It is characterized by a protracted upward trajectory and frequently signifies a reversal pattern that denotes a shift in a modest, if not enduring, upward trend (downward). Trading volume trends can also serve as an indicator to validate the strength of the signal.

Trading Opportunity: In the event that the price breaches the support line and successfully fulfills the pattern, proceed to initiate a sell order.

Bullish and Bearish Flag

Description: An aesthetically balanced, diminutive symmetrical triangle, commonly referred to as a pennant. This is typically succeeded by a pronounced upward / downward movement, subsequently leading to a brief period of price stabilization in the form of a triangular pattern (a minor alteration in direction), which confirms the existing upward / downward trend. Before (Bearish) resumes. The magnitude of the consolidation period ought to be reduced, while the breakout should occur with increased volume. In the event that no flagpole is present (abrupt ascent/descent), the object in question assumes a triangular shape rather than a pennant. Furthermore, it should be noted that pennants exhibit a transient pattern, distinct from that of a triangle.

In order to capitalize on the renewed momentum, it is essential to identify the breakouts that surpass the bullish or bearish threshold.

Rectangle

A pause in a trend is typically indicated by a rectangular shape, illustrating the unilateral price movement between the zones of support and resistance. Prior to resuming its trajectory in the initial direction, the pattern signifies the prevailing price stability of the ongoing trend (whether in an upward or downward direction).

Trade: An individual practicing swing trading has the opportunity to engage in trading the emerging rectangle pattern by purchasing assets at the designated support level and subsequently selling them when the established resistance level is reached. The Trend Trader anticipates a breakthrough in the initial trajectory of the trend, upon which the candle concludes its session near a level of support or resistance, determined by the prevailing trend. This pivotal moment informs the decision to enter the trade at the closing price of the candle.

ABCD pattern

Summary: The ABCD pattern represents recurring market-specific rhythmic patterns that traders leverage to discern potential trading prospects. The ABCD patterns are extensively utilized and formed in both bullish and bearish markets due to their efficacy across various time frames. These patterns are classified under harmonic patterns, characterized by the presence of two symmetrical value legs.

Trading: The identification of the ABCD pattern in the price chart is a straightforward task, which suggests the presence of lucrative opportunities with a high likelihood of success. They are utilized to forecast an economic downturn coming to an end.

Butterfly

Statement: The utilization of the butterfly pattern enables the recognition of the termination of price movement, thus allowing for timely market entry upon price reversal.

The Prospects And Potential Of Cryptocurrency In The Future

As the cryptocurrency landscape progresses and reaches a more advanced stage, it is only natural to ponder upon the prospects that lie ahead. An essential inquiry pertains to whether a cryptocurrency will attain extensive adoption and establish itself as a prevalent means of payment and exchange in mainstream society.

Several variables have the potential to impact the future of cryptocurrency, including the involvement of central banks and governmental entities. Certain central banks are conducting investigations into the adoption of central bank digital currencies (CBDCs), presenting the possibility of these currencies either rivaling or complementing existing forms of cryptocurrency. The future course of cryptocurrency is expected to be significantly influenced by the degree to which central banks and governments embrace or implement regulatory measures pertaining to it.

Cutting-edge technologies such as artificial intelligence and the Internet of Things may also exert a profound influence on the trajectory of cryptocurrency in the years to come. These advancements in technology possess the capacity to engender novel applications for digital currency and augment its functionalities. Nevertheless, they may also give rise to difficulties and uncertainties, notably the possibility of power consolidation within a handful of prominent entities.

Ultimately, the cryptocurrency sector will persist in encountering a multitude of pitfalls and obstacles, encompassing susceptibility to security breaches, the considerable fluctuation in valuation, and the imminent prospect of unauthorized utilization. The industry must prioritize the acknowledgment and effective management of these risks to safeguard its sustained viability and triumph.

In the subsequent and concluding section, we will present pragmatic recommendations for individuals who are keen on utilizing or investing in cryptocurrency. During our program, we will delve into various subjects including the process of purchasing and selling cryptocurrency, implementing robust security measures for its safe storage, as well as the strategies involved in creating a well-diversified cryptocurrency portfolio.

Acquisition Methods For Cryptocurrencies

Purchase Risk

Purchasing coins from unfamiliar sellers entails a potential hazard. Particularly when undertaking such actions with fiat currencies. There exists a possibility that upon payment, the transfer of the coin may not be executed. That is a risk that you must account for when selecting a broker for coin acquisition and initiating trading activities. There exists a pair of approaches to surmount this challenge. One option is to purchase the coin from a seller who is respected and trustworthy. By adopting this approach, you can ensure that the funds are successfully deposited and the coins securely arrive in your wallet. Subsequently, the next step entails transferring the funds in your wallet to a registered wallet provided by the trading broker. Subsequently, you are permitted to execute trades according to your preferences. That eliminates the potential risks associated with making the purchase. However, there is yet another risk to consider in the context of trading.

It is widely misunderstood that a variety of trading establishments exist which function on the periphery. What they do is take your coin (be it BTC, Ethereum or Monero) and they then make the purchase on the market or you. Occasionally, they abstain from completing the physical transaction and instead document the transaction in the ledger as if the purchase had taken place. This occurrence is prevalent in various brokerage firms, as it aligns with the operational practices of traditional financial brokers. These brokers typically engage in the bulk purchase of popular assets, reserving a portion for their own discretionary accounts, and subsequently allocating the remaining shares to other clients who have also acquired them.

That is acceptable, provided the system functions properly. However, on certain occasions, the broker's risk tolerance and accounting practices may prompt them to refrain from executing the purchase, opting instead for a contrary position to yours. In the event of financial loss, they offer coverage by recouping the lost funds. However, if you happen to be successful, they generally draw from their personal funds to compensate you. They are wagering on the likelihood of your losses outweighing your victories. However, complications arise when they make erroneous selections, resulting in a substantial number of their clientele benefiting from the unsuccessful trades.

That leads to a scenario where they are unable to fulfill the role and they ultimately depart.

This risk is commonly encountered by emerging brokerage firms striving for rapid success. When dealing with brokerages, it is essential to exercise intelligence. Select either a well-established brokerage or one that meets your articulated requirements for security measures.

Acquiring and counterparty exposure are indeed inherent risks within various trading landscapes, with online cryptocurrency brokerages exhibiting an even greater susceptibility to these risks. A general principle to consider is that in the event of insolvency of a brokerage firm, it is highly improbable that investors will be able to recover their lost funds. Embrace this reality and allocate only the necessary items during your interaction with them. If you intend to engage in extensive trading, it is imperative to establish the essential infrastructure for securely storing the coins that are not actively being exchanged. Considering that it is advisable to allocate no more than half of your coins for investment purposes or to diversify your investments across two distinct and unaffiliated brokerages, it becomes advantageous to dedicate your efforts to establishing an offline storage solution that ensures isolation and enhanced security measures.

Comparing Day Trading With Long-Term Investing

Several variables contribute to determining the optimal duration for executing a trade. It does not solely rely on your level of comfort or the nature of your schedule. The distinction between being a part-time day trader and a full-time one will greatly influence the range of choices available to you. Conversely, the decision will also be influenced by factors such as your capital holdings and your tenure in the market. That principle pertains to every market.

When it comes to the cryptocurrency markets, there are several additional factors that need to be considered. It is important to bear in mind that one should perceive them as a combination of assets, instead of solely regarding them as currency assets.

Cryptocurrencies, particularly BTC, possess distinct characteristics, while the altcoins exhibit different distinctive traits. We will examine each of them sequentially.

Determining whether to engage in daily trading or hold an asset for an extended period necessitates the evaluation of two key facets. The primary factor to consider pertains to the specific instrument, necessitating a thorough understanding of the asset that one plans to trade. The next aspect pertains to the infrastructure utilized by traders. We shall address both of these matters as we proceed.

When assessing the asset, one must determine its potential to offer a favorable combination of risk and reward, enabling the execution of trades that yield a positive outcome and a return on investment exceeding the norm.

What is the rationale behind your requirement for an above-average return on investment? Despite their profitability, cryptocurrencies lack inherent representation of tangible assets. They epitomize the abstract condition of interactions between two entities; yet, when such conditions are halted or seized, the asset itself ceases to exist. Imagine a barter trade. If I engage in the exchange of a group of bovine animals in return for a parcel of terrain, in the final analysis, there are tangible constituents associated with the transaction. If I were to focus on the economic aspect of that illustration and exchange a group of cows for currency, I would possess one physical asset and one monetary asset. When engaging in the process of exchanging currency, I obtain two financial assets that derive their worth from the guarantee provided by a sovereign government to uphold the stated value on the monetary bill. However, when it comes to cryptocurrencies, the worth of the coin is solely and entirely influenced by market dynamics. This represents the pinnacle of sophistication in employing mathematical and computational innovations hitherto, yet in the presence of an issue, the value of the currency dissipates entirely.

However, as commonly understood, risk is a relative concept. Additionally, there exists the possibility of the dollar experiencing a decline in value, alongside the potential occurrence of catastrophic events that could adversely impact the economic strength of the currency. It is not feasible to consider every single factor, as the abundance of data points would be overwhelming to manage. Therefore, we establish heuristic guidelines to ensure the systematic classification of particular matters as the fundamental principles. Subsequently, dynamic factors are employed in addition to assess the volatility or intraday transactions.

Allow me to provide an illustrative example that presents a more coherent understanding. Consider the hypothetical scenario wherein the North Korean currency became eligible for trade. Your initial intuition will immediately indicate that it would not be prudent to allocate all of your assets to that singular investment—if you were even considering any allocation at all. The rationale behind this is the elevated potential for depreciation and one inherently comprehends this—there exists a lack of stability in the actions or policies that the government may undertake. With the presence of such instability arises the problem of inadequate risk of cash availability and concerns pertaining to volatility.

Another aspect to consider with regard to risk is the potential for asset manipulation. This is a commonly overlooked aspect that many investors fail to take into account when selecting an investment asset.

Regardless of whether you are referring to the dollar, the won, or a digital currency such as Monero, it is imperative to consider the potential entities capable of exerting influence over its value. It might be presumed that currencies are immune to manipulation, however, one would be astounded to learn otherwise. Do you believe that the valuation of the Chinese yuan is aligned with its natural equilibrium as determined by market forces? Alternatively, are you aware that it is maintained through the application of a managed floating exchange rate system? In formal tone, the same idea can be expressed as follows: "A managed floating exchange rate regime denotes a monetary policy approach wherein the government, after careful deliberation, opts to fix the value of its currency against another currency, deeming such a pegged rate conducive to supporting the country's trade dynamics and facilitating the flow of goods and services." Several Asian countries employ this practice in order to create a more favorable environment for Western countries to access products at a more affordable price. This phenomenon gives rise to a substantial trade imbalance, fueled by the currency manipulation that arises from the deliberate pegging of the currency.

In the given illustration, the issuing nation or ruling authority of the currency possesses a significant magnitude, enabling it to bear the adverse impact resulting from the actions of sellers. Is this not manipulation?

It is. In the realm of cryptocurrencies, the absence of a centralized governing entity, akin to a sovereign government, eliminates the necessity for an artificial fixation of BTC through pegging mechanisms.

One must carefully consider these factors and determine whether they are genuinely committed to remaining in the market for an extended period of time in order to withstand such manipulation. In the immediate term, that may be acceptable, however, in the foreseeable future, it presents a substantial risk to your trading assets.

Allow me to rephrase it as follows. I would refrain from allocating a significant proportion of my available investment capital to any particular currency, including cryptocurrencies. Upon careful consideration, it becomes apparent that cryptocurrencies possess a dual capacity for generating profits. To begin with, they provide opportunities for trading in both upward and downward movements. Additionally, they provide extended periods for appreciation as they exist within different phases of adoption. As the number of individuals adopting and utilizing these coins increases, a corresponding surge in demand exerts upward pressure on the pricing of the coin. That gradual decline will eventually diminish, leading to a stabilization of pricing. One can already observe signs of this phenomenon with Bitcoin. Setting aside irrational exuberance, it is important to note that the element responsible for its rise to $17,000 cannot be considered sustainable or suitable for long-term investment purposes; however, the daily upward movements and subsequent retracement offer opportunities for daily profitability.

That allocation is exclusively dedicated to Bitcoin. The maximum duration for which you can maintain possession of this item ranges from one day up to a week, with an absolute maximum of ten days. It is advisable to exclusively engage in scalping, day trading, or swing trading Bitcoin.

When it comes to alternative cryptocurrencies, it is advisable to limit your trading activities to scalping and day trading exclusively. The altcoins presently in circulation have indeed gleaned valuable insights from Bitcoin's structural development. However, they are still relatively nascent and lack the level of established stature that Bitcoin possesses. There persist instances of unauthorized access that impede the positive price trajectory, there persist instances of theft to take into account and there persist challenges related to widespread acceptance that remain unresolved. Engaging in a day trading approach focused on altcoins - cryptocurrencies other than BTC - proves advantageous as it permits ongoing and continual trading during their ascent, while also ensuring the safety of your funds by withdrawing from the market when the day concludes.

When formulating your Bitcoin trading strategy, it is crucial to take into account the following factors that inform your mindset:

Bitcoin

Devoid of an underlying asset

Liquid

Characterized by significant price fluctuations ranging from 4 to 8% on a daily basis.

These three factors influence your BTC trading decision towards becoming a potential candidate for day trading or swing trading. This is due to the fact that, even if you adhere to a twelve-hour trading day, you will have the opportunity to capitalize on both upward movements and retracements, thus potentially yielding higher profits than if you were to simply acquire a position and hold it.

Let me illustrate.

I shall exemplify a standard day of cryptocurrency trading, devoid of any significant market fundamental news, for illustrative purposes.

Suppose that the initial price of the coin is 10000 per USD. I employ approximate numbers to enhance the clarity and simplicity of the computations being conveyed. Throughout the course of the day, the value of the coin fluctuates between the ranges of 10000 and 10800. That represents an appreciation of 8%; however, not all of us possess the necessary precision to enter the market precisely at its lowest point and exit at its highest. For the purpose of providing an example, let us assume that this constitutes the upper limit of your earning potential—should you engage in a singular trade.

However, that is not the correct approach to engage in this game. You are engaging in cryptocurrency trading as a result of its inherent volatility and liquidity, with the purpose of capitalizing on upward price movements and tactfully exiting positions when a retracement occurs. Please find below a visual representation of how that would appear.

If one were to initiate a trade at a market entry point of 10050, and subsequently observe a rise to 10200 followed by a subsequent decline, it would be advisable to execute the liquidation of the initial position established earlier in the day at a level such as 10180. That's a $130 profit.

Allow it to reach the lowest point of the retracement, and remain patient until it reverses direction and begins ascending again. After remounting, let us assume that the value ascends to 10000 and subsequently reverses its trajectory. You have the option to board the vehicle at 10020 and subsequently take it back up to the point where it makes a turn at 10200. At this juncture, you may disembark, if you so choose, once again at the 10200 location. Subsequently, you allow it to descend and subsequently, it proceeds to reach 10150 before subsequently reversing direction and subsequently, you intercept it at 10170.

You capitalize on the upward momentum of the wave, carrying you to a peak of 10330, prior to gradually receding. You strategically exit at the level of 10300, just as it begins its descent towards 10240, subsequently positioning itself for another rise. You embark at the station numbered 10280 and proceed on the journey until reaching station 10430, at which point it commences its reversal. Subsequently, you receive the indication to initiate a leap at 10400 as it descends to 10340, prior to its subsequent ascent where you successfully intercept it at 10360.

At this juncture, you continue the course until reaching the subsequent crest. The event occurs at a value of 10480, and subsequently you proceed with the liquidation process at a value of 10460. It progresses up to 10400 prior to retracing its path, at which point you intercept it at 10420 and proceed to traverse it until reaching 10550. Similarly, you proceed with the subsequent trades. Purchased at a valuation of 10,530, sold at 10,650; procured at 10,630, and sold at 10,750; acquired at 10,730, and yielded at 10,800.

"Altogether, this is the overall outcome you achieved:

In the initial transaction, a profit of 180 was achieved (from 10020 to 10200). Subsequently, the same pattern was repeated in successive trades, resulting in profits of 180 (from 10020 to 10200), 130 (from 10170 to 10300), 150 (from

10280 to 10430), 100 (from 10360 to 10460), 130 (from 10420 to 10550), 120 (from 10530 to 10650), 120 (from 10630 to 10750), and 70 (from 10730 to 10800). The grand total amounts to $1180. Thus, rather than solely earning $800 on the single trade, you capitalized on the trajectory of the cryptocurrency's upward movement, seizing the opportunity as it experienced a retracement and subsequent rally. Nevertheless, that result falls short of the most favorable outcome. There is still one better way. One possible way to approach this is by capitalizing on market downturns, in addition to launching attacks on the market.

Allow me to present a visual representation of the concept:

Upon reaching the summit of the run, where one proceeds to liquidate their initial long position, they simultaneously execute a short order. When you do this, you will be able to scalp the market on its retracements.

Allow me to elucidate the subsequent course of events:

Simply include an supplementary order ticket to your trades. Upon commencement, you initiated at the value of 10020 and proceeded to divest at the price of 10200. In conjunction with the liquidation directive, it is advisable to place a supplementary sales instruction at a price of 10200. You close out that particular position when you enter the market, ensuring that your subsequent buying position is set at 10020. As you initiate a purchase at the price of 10020, you concurrently execute the liquidation of the aforementioned short sale.

This will result in a net profit of 180 for the short sale. Afterwards, enact your purchase as previously mentioned, at a price point of 10020, and subsequently divest at 10200. Attached herewith is your liquidation order, along with a newly generated sell order for 10200. This will result in an additional 180 units of profit. Similarly, you are presently engaging in shorting whenever you liquidate your position.

And here is an illustration of what that entails:

The initial short position in our trade is projected to result in a gain of 180 (from 10200 to 10020). The subsequent transaction will result in an additional 180 units (reducing the count from 10,200 to 10,020). The third trade will be executed at a price of 10200 and subsequently closed at a price of 10170, resulting in a net gain of 30 units of currency. The fourth transaction commences at the price of 10300 and concludes at 10280, resulting in a profit of 20 units. The fifth transaction commences at 10430 and concludes at 10360, resulting in a gain of 130. The sixth transaction commences at a price of 10460 and concludes at a price of 10420, resulting in a profit of 40. The subsequent figure is 10550, followed by an exit at 10530 with a profit of 20. Subsequently, the next step entails proceeding to 10650, followed by a subsequent movement towards 10630, resulting in a difference of 20. Next, the value reaches 10750 and concludes at 10730, resulting in a difference of 20. Overall, this amounts to a supplementary profit of $640 instead of solely purchasing during periods of price increase.

The cumulative value of your long positions amounts to $1180, whereas your short positions are expected to yield $640, resulting in a combined total of $1820.

Consider the advantages that arise from the prospect of engaging in a cryptocurrency featuring a market characterized by both volatility and liquidity. You possess the capacity to capitalize on the ascending movement, and likewise, stand the chance to generate profits during the descending phase. Overall, your earnings amount to $1820, as opposed to a mere $600 from a single trade.

If you perceive this as a significant workload, it is worth noting that specialized software exists to facilitate the purchasing and selling process based on your customized patterns and instructions. Therefore, the aforementioned approach can be readily inputted into a trading program and implemented. In the case of the software, it shall adhere to the designated entry and exit points stipulated by the user, subsequently carrying out the trading operations. One must simply oversee and ensure that it refrains from engaging in any conduct that may lead to adverse consequences. I organize all of my programs in a manner that prompts trade recommendations and awaits my endorsement, subsequently executing them only upon my approval. In the event that the interval between the proposition and my endorsement is excessively protracted, resulting in the expiration of the opportunity, my software undergoes recalculation to furnish me with an alternative option.

I will present a few additional alternatives that you may consider incorporating into your strategies at a later point within the book. They will provide you with an orientation on initiating and implementing your personal trading strategies, or at the very least, offer you guidance on the approach to take. Engaging in the trading of cryptocurrencies provides a significant level of autonomy and space for ingenuity, enabling the execution of highly refined trades similar to the one we have recently witnessed.

DeFi and Business Models

The singular benefit offered by this platform lies in its rating system, which facilitates the verification of reliability for all involved parties. Additionally, it ensures a substantial level of traffic for all involved parties. Renters can rest assured that they will consistently have a wide array of properties available for selection in any location, while landlords can have confidence that their properties will consistently attract a substantial number of renters through the platform.

Nevertheless, these advantageous circumstances are in place due to the absence of alternative feasible solutions. Now, let us examine the fees levied by Airbnb in return for these advantages. Homeowners incur a fee amounting to approximately three percent of the booking price, derived from the funds paid by renters. A mere three percent may not appear consequential, yet let us consider the broader context. When engaging the services of a real estate agent to purchase a property, a commission fee of four percent is levied on the sale.

The real estate agent possesses a substantial workload. The individual in question is responsible for curating a comprehensive inventory of properties, diligently overseeing the documentation process, facilitating the escrow arrangement, adeptly advocating for the interests of either the buyer or seller, and effectively disseminating vital information to all relevant stakeholders.

What precise actions does Airbnb undertake that approximate such outcomes? It is the remunerated edition of the property category on Craigslist. Indeed, during its formative years,

Airbnb developed an API access point to infiltrate the exclusive listings segment of Craigslist, thereby redirecting traffic from the aforementioned website. This is regarded as an exemplary manifestation of growth hacking in Silicon Valley. In the context of any rational individual in society, this can be perceived as an uncomplicated act of misappropriating the assets belonging to another enterprise.

No fees are imposed on the tenants. Nevertheless, this phenomenon can be attributed to the fact that the renter plays the role of the commodity. The tenant provides Airbnb with valuable data, which the platform utilizes to reintroduce services to the market and recommend alternative property listings. The platform constructs a comprehensive user profile containing personally identifiable information as well as credit card details that may potentially be susceptible to unauthorized access. In the event of a data breach, Airbnb assumes no liability for any resulting damages. In the event of Airbnb being acquired by corporate entities such as Google or Amazon in the future, it is plausible for these organizations to possess comprehensive knowledge regarding one's personal affairs. Surpassing the quality of your familial relations.

What could potentially be the operational mechanisms of a decentralized application serving a similar purpose as Airbnb?

DApps

Let us designate our Decentralized Application as 'DAirbnb'. This application is built upon the blockchain technology, utilizing a network of interconnected Smart Contracts. To begin with, the application would facilitate a review platform wherein all users can corroborate one another's conduct and past performance. Does tenant ownership present a favorable proposition? Does the prospective tenant possess qualities that deem them suitable for tenancy? All individuals possess the capability to submit photographs showcasing their possessions, although they are under no obligation to divulge personal images if they so choose.

The filters pertaining to Wi-Fi, laptop-compatible workstations, and laundry facilities will be present on Airbnb. Indeed, the interface will bear an exact resemblance to that of Airbnb. The disparity lies entirely within the internal mechanics. When engaging in communication through the application, one can rest assured that their messages and interactions do not undergo storage within a database. They are securely retained within a ledger implemented through blockchain technology. The messages possess cryptographic signatures, rendering them invulnerable to hacking attempts.

Only you and the proprietor have the ability to access and peruse those communications. Furthermore, it is conveniently possible to exchange contact information. Airbnb prohibits its users from engaging in this activity due to the potential consequences of establishing an offline agreement between the involved parties. This impedes the generation of revenue for the platform. Nevertheless, the DApp remains indifferent to this aspect as the reward for engaging with it far surpasses that of in-person interaction.

Reputation

A decentralized application lacks a singular governing authority. This implies that the review system holds greater significance in the current context. The greater the number of reviews a user possesses, the more enhanced their experience is likely to be. Now, let us proceed to the next level. Could it be proposed that DAirbnb is merely a singular application situated upon a blockchain infrastructure comprising numerous additional applications?

There could potentially exist a digital platform DGrocery that facilitates the online purchase of essential groceries, a transportation service DUber for commuting purposes, and a platform DStylist catering to various personal care needs, among others. An entire ecosystem of applications that gather feedback from diverse users who can vouch for your character based on their interactions with you. In the event that you have not previously engaged in renting accommodations through DAirbnb, it is of utmost importance to note that owners within the platform possess the ability to access your reviews derived from past interactions within the ecosystem.

If a centralized system were to assume control, this would result in a dystopian nightmare. Nevertheless, all data and interactions are stored on the blockchain, providing users with complete autonomy and control over their information. Please disclose your desires while abstaining from sharing any other information. In the event that another user requires confidential information (according to your specified definition), you have the option to securely transmit it to them, with the assurance that they will not misuse it. That information will not be stored within a database that is susceptible to unauthorized access. Thus, the process of effectively managing and cultivating a reputation on DAirbnb is considerably more convenient compared to embarking upon the same endeavor through traditional offline means.

Identity verification

When discussing blockchain, individuals frequently raise the initial objection that it is impossible to authenticate an individual's identity. As you have acquired knowledge, it is evident that this is an inaccurate statement. Adversaries of blockchain often portray it as a platform that enables individuals to adopt any identity of their choosing. Nevertheless, this is not the modus operandi of blockchain technology.

Users are granted the autonomy to verify the identity of another individual according to their own discretion.

It is simply the case that identity is marginalized and this reality is difficult to accept. Furthermore, the manner in which blockchain applications authenticate identity diverges from that of a centralized application. For instance, Airbnb provides the option to present the individual's name and additional details. In general, this poses no significant risks as individuals seldom disclose confidential information. Nonetheless, in order to authenticate your identity, Airbnb gathers personal information from delicate documents such as passports and identification cards. The modus operandi of an identity verification protocol on the blockchain operates in a distinct manner. Fundamentally, it is a contractual agreement utilizing Smart Contract technology that is entered into by two parties. The contract establishes a legal framework between the two parties, serving to authenticate the identities of both entities involved. Neither party shall be provided with any sensitive information or any information beyond that which the other party is willing to disclose.

Suppose you are in the process of reserving a room on DAirbnb and the host expresses an interest in verifying your identity. Airbnb employs a technologically advanced SmartID protocol, which functions as an autonomous application on the blockchain to ensure utmost security while verifying your identity. Once more, there is no risk of a hacking incident or cyber-attack. You are required to provide the host with your photograph and full name, concluding the information-sharing process.

In reciprocation, you may verify the presence of a suitable physical accommodation provided by the host, ensuring the absence of any unauthorized imitation or suspicious activities. The outcome is a system that possesses significantly enhanced security in comparison to conventional Airbnb practices. The decentralized application is entirely reliant on peer participation and fosters enhanced trust among individuals, even in light of the minimal disclosure of personal information.

Contrast this with an offline transaction wherein one must physically present their identification and have it manually verified by an authorized individual. The utilization of blockchain technology provides a significantly enhanced level of security, which serves as a compelling motivation.

Risk Management

Centralized databases are susceptible to unauthorized disclosures, breaches, and illicit transactions to the most competitive bidder. Decentralized applications do not centralize information storage. There is a stark disparity between the security provided by the blockchain and that offered by any alternative solution.

Insurance

Airbnb provides property owners with an insurance coverage of $1 million to safeguard against potential damages and theft. It is among the limited number of factors that contribute to the platform's value. From a skeptical perspective, one could argue that it is merely a tactic to absolve themselves of responsibility; nevertheless, the existence of insurance provides owners with a sense of assurance.

A decentralized application would afford an equivalent level of safeguarding while exhibiting heightened efficacy. Airbnb would merely implement an additional protocol, referred to as DAssurance, wherein multiple insurers would have access to tenant and landlord data and be able to tailor quotes according to each party's specific circumstances.

In this manner, upstanding tenants will be able to enjoy reduced insurance premiums, whereas tenants with unfavorable reputations will bear higher costs. Landlords can have peace of mind knowing that their specific requirements are addressed. Please be aware that the evaluation of risk is not influenced by an individual's identity. It solely relies on their transaction history on DAirbnb.

Insurers will not be necessitated to obtain substantiation of your identity or any other confidential information in order to authenticate your identity. The pertinent data is readily accessible on the network, and it only requires them to retrieve the transaction records that are publicly accessible. The insurance agreement may be transmitted as an alternative Smart Contract which encompasses all individuals involved and benefits from a multi-signature security mechanism.

Therefore, the entire experience is centered around peer interaction, with DAirbnb providing support in facilitating those connections. It does not reside centrally, merely collecting rental fees for providing you the privilege of facilitating a connection to another location.

Payments

This represents a significant benefit derived from the utilization of a DApp. Landlords do not experience lengthy delays in receiving funds, as the availability of funds is immediate. Tenants frequently voice dissatisfaction with regards to the arbitrary retention of security deposits. Indeed, an effective solution to this predicament is the implementation of a Smart Contract designed to hold the deposit funds in escrow. Indeed, a deposit will not be necessitated with regards to a lease of extended duration.

The lease in question will be implemented as a smart contract. In the event that the tenant does not adhere to the provisions, the agreement will, on its own, indemnify the landlord for any resulting harm. All substantiating data and evidence in favor of the assertions and documentation of the initial terms can be appended to the contract, allowing for verification by all involved parties.

In the event of a contention, an unbiased arbitrator may be granted authorization to examine the issue and facilitate its resolution. In the event that the dispute proceeds to litigation, neither party is afforded the opportunity to modify or exploit the circumstances, given that an indisputable record of events is maintained. The outcome entails a more secure and streamlined experience for all participating parties.

Access

An issue that arises in the monetization of a property on Airbnb is the infrequency with which guests are able to check in. Advances in computer technology have reached a stage where ordinary devices are now capable of autonomous operation or can be seamlessly controlled via a mobile application. Smart locks are currently accessible; nevertheless, achieving automation of their features poses a challenge.

For instance, landlords have the capability to activate smart locks for granting access to individuals. However, they are required to physically ascertain the alignment between the guest's information and the details provided on the platform.

The utilization of Smart Contracts enables the automation of the entire process via the blockchain. The parameters of a smart contract can be interconnected with a smart lock. When the guest reaches the lock, they have the option to present an electronically encoded key contained within the smart contract. In the event that the key is a valid match, the door shall be successfully unlocked and the guest shall proceed with the check-in process.

This approach enables the consolidation of the entire rental workflow within a single smart contract. Landowners are able to effectively control their properties from a remote location, with the assurance that their properties remain safeguarded and immune to any form of manipulation. It mitigates the influence that a property management company may exert on the taxation and income derived by the landlord.

Blockchain

It is widely understood that blockchain functions as a decentralized database in which transactions can be securely stored. Blockchain may be perceived as the fundamental underpinning that facilitates the existence of technologies such as cryptocurrency. Blockchain technology autonomously acquires data and disseminates it across an extensive network of decentralized nodes, thus enabling the global broadcast of said data. The network operates on a decentralized peer-to-peer framework, employing robust cryptographic techniques and digital signatures to ensure seamless execution of transactions.

Each newly created block incorporates a chain that comprises details pertaining to various transactions and smart contracts, along with interconnected information that establishes its linkage to adjacent blocks. A timestamp is additionally employed to enable the chain to promptly ascertain its position within the entirety of the network. The verification of each block in the network will be conducted by external block miners. The inclusion of blocks in the chain as a whole is contingent upon verification by the miners.

Miners endeavor to decipher proof-of-work systems, wherein their objective entails unraveling intricate mathematical equations employing equipment purposely engineered for this specific purpose. The equations safeguard the network against security breaches by mitigating service attacks and ensuring uninterrupted functionality.

Miners are rewarded based on the cryptocurrency they have mined and the collective effort exerted by the participants involved in completing the selected mining block. The majority of the presently available cryptocurrencies impose a nominal transaction fee, a fraction of which is allocated to the miners themselves.

The data housed within the blockchain technology is protected due to the inherent design of the blockchain system.

Blockchain Technology

The rising popularity of blockchain technology can be attributed to its manifold transformative effects on various aspects of business operations, daily routines, the realm of cryptocurrency, and the dynamics between governments, lawmakers, and the wider population.

Applications in the Business Sector
Money transfer and payments.

Although commonly associated with cryptocurrency transactions, blockchain technology possesses the capacity to transcend its current boundaries by efficiently addressing the multifaceted needs of enterprises, enabling them to harness the full spectrum of its capabilities. The Ethereum Enterprise Alliance (EEA) is a consortium consisting of prominent corporations such as Samsung, JP Morgan, and Microsoft, collaborating to develop a blockchain platform utilizing Ethereum technology, while also incorporating the necessary degree of governance required for seamless utilization by businesses.

This kind of service is observable in various regions across the globe. More people in Kenya are currently using the bitcoin wallet which has indoor plumbing. Facilitating the integration of these emerging participants into the realm of the internet will yield favorable consequences for retailers on a global scale.

Notary services.

Blockchain technology possesses the capacity to effectively supplant conventional notary services. There exists a multitude of applications accessible on the internet that can be utilized for the purpose of notarizing various forms of content.

Cold storage.

Nowadays, blockchain technology has the capability to serve as a platform for facilitating the connection between users and cloud storage resources, much like how Airbnb operates. Individuals who possess unutilized surplus storage capacity on their hard drives can opt to lease out said excess space to individuals who require supplementary storage capacity. The estimated valuation of cloud storage exceeds $20 billion, presenting a significant and lucrative business prospect.

Fraud

Blockchain technology possesses the capability to effectively trace and identify online identities. The system is deemed to be both safe and secure. Blockchain has the potential to resolve the aforementioned matter due to its capacity to produce outcomes that are duly verified, safeguarded, indisputable, and unchangeable. This enhancement in the system eradicates intricate password or dual-factor authentication mechanisms, and instead implements a system that will ultimately rely on digital signatures and cryptography to ensure the safety and security of all users.

Through the utilization of blockchain technology, the transaction will undergo processing akin to that of a conventional transaction. The sole verification needed will be to ascertain the origin of the funds and confirm that they correspond to the account of the individual who authorized the aforementioned transaction. Similar technology is currently being utilized to process birth certificates, residency forms, physical identification, and passports. There exist applications that leverage blockchain technology to authenticate the identity of users through their mobile devices.

Communication within the Supply Chain
Blockchain technology facilitates the seamless monitoring of deliveries by companies, subsequently enabling the automated initiation of payment upon the successful receipt of products by the intended recipients.

Gift Cards

Distributing gift cards is an effective marketing tactic, yet in the end, a minor portion of customers actually utilize them. Blockchain technology has the potential to revolutionize this by establishing a direct connection between customers and loyalty offers, thereby facilitating the secure verification and real-time updating of pertinent information, much like a digital gift card. The interconnected network of physical devices, commonly referred to as the "Internet of Things",

A distributed ledger technology that serves as a publicly accessible registry for multiple devices? Autonomous Decentralized Peer-to-Peer Telemetry, abbreviated as ADEPT, encapsulates the fundamental principles and objectives we aim to achieve. It is a system of proof-of-concept that has been jointly developed by Microsoft and Samsung. The ADEPT system leverages blockchain technology to serve as the underlying infrastructure. It leveraged the file-sharing capability of BitTorrent, the smart contract technology of Ethereum, and the peer-to-peer messaging functionality of TeleHash to substantiate the underlying concept.

The blockchain implemented within the ADEPT system functions as a register of occurrences for all the devices engaging in independent broadcast transactions amidst a hierarchical system of peer devices and architecture.

Insurance Contracts

Smart contracts have the capacity to revolutionize the insurance industry. Rather than engaging with insurance agents who must still ascertain responsibility in the event of a work-related injury, the blockchain will utilize micro-contract business payments. The implementation of blockchain technology will result in a more efficient and seamless claims process, leading to enhanced customer experiences and substantial cost savings for the company.

Funding

A decentralized application operating on the Ethereum blockchain offers small businesses the opportunity to access credit. Benefactors have the option to utilize the application for transmitting digital currency funds to their designated recipients. The funds will undergo conversion to the currency designated for the intended recipient and will be disbursed through a proprietary transaction mechanism. They offer loans without any collateral requirements with a guarantee of 100% security, while also providing a range of comprehensive training and consulting services.

Microblogging

In the context of a technologically-driven society, enterprises persist in seeking effective measures to facilitate seamless interaction with their intended demographic. In contemporary times, there is a notable surge in the popularity of blogging. Consequently, certain service providers have introduced decentralized microblogging services that operate on the Ethereum blockchain. The service bears resemblance to Twitter; however, it operates on a decentralized system, thereby eliminating any imposed limitations on users' postings and refraining from filtering of transmitted messages.

Applications in Everyday Scenarios
Healthcare
The objective is to establish a connection between individuals and their healthcare information for the purpose of accessing medical care at the hospital when necessary. Preliminary evaluation indicates that this novel concept has the potential to decrease the occurrence of medical errors.

Internet Decentralization

Google has contributed to the process of centralization on the internet. Blockstack is committed to altering this situation. It grants individuals unrestricted access to the functionalities of blockchain technology, enabling them to participate in an internet framework wherein users exert full authority over their personal data. This system will function similarly to the conventional internal system; however, it eliminates the need for users to create multiple accounts for various websites. Instead, users will have a singular primary account and can grant temporary access to specific accounts. Once you have completed the task, you may proceed to formally disassociate a particular website from your account.

Blockstack offers a cryptographic ledger system that maintains records of usernames and varying degrees of encryption.

Improved Property Rights

Company shares and patents encompass both physical and non-physical assets, ranging from tangible properties such as cars to intangible assets like intellectual property rights. All of the components will be linked together through the implementation of a smart contract and blockchain technology. The relevant contractual details are securely stored within a decentralized ledger. The ledger possesses the capacity to meticulously monitor minor intricacies and trigger targeted actions as necessary.

Emerging Forms of Financial Service Providers

The advent of blockchain technology has greatly enhanced the convenience of fund transfers. An evidence to substantiate this claim is the emergence of hard money lenders, typically characterized by their exorbitant interest rates. Utilizing blockchain technology for lending purposes may necessitate a decreased reliance on collateral and enable the utilization of smaller contractual agreements, subsequently leading to a reduction in costs.

Smartphones

Contemporary mobile devices now possess biometric authentication functionalities such as fingerprint and facial recognition applications, which can be categorically referred to as cryptographic techniques. The implementation of blockchain technology will provide an additional layer of enhancement to this security feature. Alternatively, rather than utilizing the physical SIM card on your smartphone as a means of storage, you have the option to store data on the blockchain, granting you access to it from any location.

Passports

A subset of individuals has been employing blockchain technology for the purpose of administering their passports. The procedure involves capturing your image and subsequently encrypting it using both a private key and a public key. The passport shall be recorded within a publicly available ledger, accessible to you through the utilization of your designated key.

Identification

In the present day, it is necessary to carry essential identification documents such as driver's license, identification card, or social security number, among various others, on our person at all times. Employing blockchain technology will facilitate your transition towards integrating digital identification technology.

Altering the Method by Which You Obtain Your Fuel

Contemporary electric vehicles have the potential to transform your lifestyle. Blockchain technology has the capability to accurately record and monitor the allocation of electricity to users, subsequently authorizing the automatic deduction of funds from the respective user's account. The user simply needs to proceed to a charging station, at which point the blockchain will assume responsibility for the subsequent proceedings.

Utilizing Blockchain Technology: Exploring Cryptocurrency and its Numerous Applications

Blockchain applications possess significant potential. It possesses the potential to transcend the realm of Bitcoin and cryptocurrencies. Based on the aforementioned applications, it is evident that this tool can effectively promote transparency and equity, resulting in significant time and cost savings for businesses. Blockchain technology is proving to have a profound influence on diverse sectors, manifesting in manners that are within the realm of one's imagination.

Below, we present several practical applications of blockchain technology in various industries.

Money Transfers

Money transfers conducted through the utilization of blockchain technology eradicate bureaucratic processes, as the implementation of ledger systems facilitates instantaneous transfers, thereby diminishing overhead charges associated with intermediaries. Blockchain technology has the potential to achieve annual cost savings of $8 to

$12 billion for large financial institutions.

Algorand

Algoorand is diligently engaged in developing a technological solution aimed at addressing the disparities that exist between conventional and decentralized finance. By enhancing protocols, their objective is to enhance the accessibility of financial transactions for all individuals.

Gemini

Gemini is a reputable platform for the trading and custodianship of digital assets, providing a regulated and secure environment for transactions involving cryptocurrencies such as Bitcoin and Ethereum. They offer a cryptographic rewards system that enables users to generate a return of up to 7.4%, which is then deposited into their digital wallets.

Smart Contracts

Smart contracts bear resemblance to conventional contracts, albeit with the distinctive feature of timely enforcement through the utilization of blockchain technology. It obviates the necessity of an intermediary, resulting in cost and time savings for businesses, while concurrently guaranteeing compliance of all involved parties.

BurstIQ

BurstIQ operates within the healthcare sector. It utilizes advanced data analytics and blockchain-based contracts to facilitate the secure transmission of sensitive healthcare data between patients and medical professionals. They have established parameters regarding the extent of information that can be shared. They additionally offer individualized healthcare plan information for patients.

MEDIACHAIN

Mediachain facilitates the remuneration of musicians by leveraging smart contracts. Upon entering into a contract that is characterized by decentralization and transparency, artists possess the ability to engage in negotiations that pertain to securing elevated royalty rates and ensuring full compensation. In April 2017, Spotify acquired Mediachain.

Internet of Things

The Internet of Things, commonly referred to as IoT, is regarded as a pivotal advancement within the realm of blockchain technology. The Internet of Things encompasses a multitude of applications on a massive scale. The proliferation of Internet of Things (IoT) devices provides cybercriminals with opportunities to compromise your personal data accessed through websites. By integrating blockchain technology into Internet of Things (IoT) systems, a heightened level of security is achieved, effectively mitigating the risk of data breaches. This is made possible by leveraging the inherent attributes of transparency and virtual incorruptibility within the application, resulting in the augmentation of 'smart' capabilities.

Filament

Filament possesses software and microchip hardware which enable interconnected devices to function on a blockchain platform. Filament employs encryption to secure ledger data and shares live data with other interconnected machines utilizing blockchain technology, thereby enabling the monetization of machines through timestamp-based mechanisms.

HYPRR

HYPR effectively mitigates cybersecurity breaches in IoT devices through the implementation of decentralized credential solutions. Passwords are retrieved from a centralized server and subsequently supplemented with biometric and password-less measures to enhance security, resulting in IoT devices exhibiting near-impenetrability.

Xage Security

Xage Security represents a pioneering blockchain-empowered cybersecurity platform that has been exclusively developed to cater to the unique requirements of Internet of Things (IoT) enterprises. It effectively handles a vast number of devices concurrently. It facilitates self-assessment and autonomous recovery in the event of security breaches. Xage Security is employed by IoT enterprises operating in the energy, manufacturing, and transportation sectors.

Personal Identity

According to the identity theft specialist LifeLock, a staggering number of over 16 million individuals in the United States fell victim to the perils of identity fraud and theft solely in the year 2017.

Ligero

Ligero provides the versatility of lightweight and expandable protocols, specifically designed for the purposes of zero-knowledge proofs and secure multiparty computation. It offers a robust framework for decentralized cooperation across both blockchain and off-blockchain environments, facilitating fully anonymous transactions, protected auctions, confidential microcontracts, and fostering verifiable machine-learning capabilities.

CIVC

Civic provides individuals with valuable insights concerning the accessability of their personal information. Civic users engage in smart contract agreements, enabling them to exercise control over the individuals authorized to access their personal data. In the event of a contract violation or an unauthorized entity attempting to access confidential information, prompt notifications are promptly sent to the user.

Numerous companies have adopted the utilization of blockchain technology for purposes that extend beyond its original scope. As we enter the year 2022, anticipate that other industries will similarly take this course of action.

Introduction

The financial realm has been significantly altered by the advent of technology. Presently, there exists a multitude of platforms, payment alternatives, and commodities that facilitate financial transactions for individuals worldwide. An exemplary instance of such technological advancements within the realm of the financial industry is the emergence of cryptocurrency. The advent of digital currency can be traced back to its early beginnings when it held minimal significance. Currently, it has witnessed substantial growth that has captured the interest of potential investors.

This literary piece serves as a comprehensive and systematic manual elucidating the intricate mechanics underlying the functioning of cryptocurrencies. If you possess prior knowledge of cryptocurrency, you are about to delve into it further, approaching it from the standpoint of a beginner. There is considerable speculation regarding the modus operandi of cryptocurrency, with individuals expressing interest in understanding its workings and long-term viability. Can anyone invest? What considerations should be given to the potential hazards? These inquiries give the impression that cryptocurrency is a highly intricate concept.

Whilst there may be certain technical terminology that you must familiarize yourself with, dedicating your attention to each specific detail within the process will enable you to comprehend the crucial elements and succeed as a cryptocurrency investor, purchaser, or vendor. In the following chapters, you will be introduced to comprehensive insights regarding cryptocurrency, the process of mining, blockchain technology, and even expert advice on trading.

It is anticipated that upon reaching the conclusion of this literary work, you will acquire a profound understanding of pertinent knowledge and acquirement of invaluable tools. These acquired assets will effectively guide and empower you to exercise sound judgment in the realm of investment. Although the cryptocurrency market exhibits volatility, substantial investments can still result in remarkable rewards.

It is imperative to acknowledge that the trajectory of cryptocurrencies is an ongoing, perpetual endeavor. Our comprehension of cryptos half a decade ago now bears no semblance to the current landscape. Engaging in a constant quest for up-to-date information shall facilitate your ability to remain at the forefront of this technological advancement.

We have reached the saturation point with the initial discussions; it is now imperative to commence proceedings. The initial chapter delves into the historical origins of cryptocurrency, providing a necessary foundation to grasp its current and future implications. In order to comprehend the present and anticipate the future, it is imperative to gain insight into the bygone era. Please proceed to the subsequent chapter and commence immediately.

1. Employment with cryptocurrencies

The surge in the popularity of cryptocurrencies has led to the emergence of numerous employment opportunities that are contingent upon possessing the requisite skill sets crucial for making substantial contributions in the realm of digital currencies. Employment opportunities within the domain of cryptocurrencies primarily pertain to technology-related roles that necessitate proficiency in various technical skills. Within the ensuing section, you shall discover a collection of positions presently accessible in the cryptocurrency market.

Although these skills may appear to be in demand

Not only are there opportunities available for individuals with technical expertise, but there are also prospects accessible to those without a technical background. The employers enhance the cryptocurrency process through the application of their invaluable soft skills, including but not limited to creativity, problem-solving capabilities, self-motivation, effective communication, and strong teamwork abilities.

There has been an upward trend observed in the cryptocurrency job market in recent times. Specifically, between 2017 and 2018, a substantial surge was witnessed in the availability of employment opportunities within the cryptocurrency sector. Upon perusing the following compilation, you are likely to come across employment opportunities within the cryptocurrency industry, enabling you to pursue a career in the realm of digital currencies.

Occupation in the realm of digital currency

1. Professional in the field of Data Science

Professionals specialized in the field of data science possess the expertise to assist organizations in analyzing transactional data that engineers, focused on optimizing experiences, can benefit from. Blockchain technology remains relatively nascent and frequently misconstrued; the task involves establishing a seamless liaison between the clientele and the technology's proficient engineers.

2. Reporter

A journalist plays a crucial role within the realm of cryptocurrencies, as they diligently report on the most recent developments concerning digital currencies and blockchain technology. Journalists of this caliber have the ability to provide coverage for a variety of media outlets, including newspapers, magazines, blogs, and technology brands that are contemplating investing in cryptocurrencies.

3. Manager of Marketing Department

In order for cryptocurrencies to achieve success, it is imperative that prospective users and investors acquire awareness of their existence as well as a comprehensive understanding of their mechanism. The responsibility of the marketing manager revolves around assessing the market demand for cryptocurrencies and blockchain technology, as well as conducting a comparative analysis of their value. Additionally, marketing managers engage in the identification of prospective users and the formulation of strategies aimed at assisting individuals in optimizing their market presence.

4. Analyst specializing in research

Given that cryptocurrency is a nascent industry, it is essential to engage research analysts to facilitate the education of prospective users regarding the advancements within this domain. This will assist them in deriving sound decisions concerning cryptocurrency matters. A research analyst is required to demonstrate strategic thinking and possess strong written communication skills.

5. Architect specialized in security

Security architects ensure that the integrity of cryptocurrency security is consistently upheld. The job responsibilities also encompass the development of safeguards aimed at safeguarding the organization's technological assets from cyber risks and deceptive transactions.

6. Professional in website development

The job entails the composition and upkeep of coded smart contracts, enabling transactions to occur without the involvement of intermediaries. Web developers have at their disposal several frequently utilized programming languages, namely JavaScript, Python, and Solidity.

7. Professional documentation author

The corporations that develop novel cryptocurrencies produce a comprehensive technical document, commonly referred to as a white paper, with the aim of enticing potential investors. Typically ranging from 20 to 50 pages in length, these white papers expound upon the company's technological progress and delineate its strategies for development and market promotion. In order to secure this position, it is imperative for individuals to possess a profound comprehension of blockchain technology, alongside exceptional proficiency in written communication.

8. Engineer specializing in machine learning

The machine learning engineer facilitates the realization of cryptocurrency's functionalities for users. The responsibilities of this position also involve developing digital applications that prioritize user-experience while ensuring their safety and security. Coinbase employs machine learning techniques to safeguard against unauthorized intrusions by hackers.

9. Financial consultant" or "Economic advisor

In order to construct a portfolio, cryptocurrency companies will necessitate the services of hedge funds, insurance providers, and engagement with private investors. The involvement of a financial analyst will be imperative in the oversight of these activities. The financial analysts are required to possess a license issued by the financial industry regulatory authority and must demonstrate comprehension of recent regulatory protocols.

10. Commercial development executive

With the emergence of novel opportunities and platforms within the crypto industry, the exigency arises for the presence of a business development representative, whose primary duty entails the facilitation of deal closures, cultivation of fresh partnerships, and promotion of products. The business development representative is also responsible for ensuring the successful implementation of business plans.

In order for an individual to procure employment within a burgeoning industry, it is imperative that they engage in extensive research and diligently follow current advancements and declarations, as these sources will furnish them with pertinent information to enhance their job prospects.

Through the act of enrolling in weekly or monthly job notifications, individuals are able to avail themselves of professional guidance pertaining to the acquisition of new employment within their specific industry.

Without a proficient understanding of trading and investment, the effective execution of any cryptocurrency-related task would be unattainable. For this reason, I would recommend proceeding to the subsequent section, wherein you will acquire comprehensive insight into the art of trading and investing in cryptocurrencies.

Computation And The State Of Being Turing-Complete

It is worth noting that the Ethereum virtual machine possesses the characteristic of being Turing-complete. By virtue of this property, the code executed on the EVM has the capacity to represent and carry out any possible computation, even those involving infinite iterations. The EVM code facilitates the utilization of looping through two distinct approaches. Firstly, there exists a JUMP instruction that enables the program to return to a previous point in the code, coupled with a JUMPI instruction for conditional jumping, which facilitates the execution of statements such as "while x".

Polygon, also recognized as MATIC in the realm of cryptocurrency, is an Indian-based blockchain scalability platform referred to as the Internet of Blockchains on the Ethereum network. MATIC serves as the digital currency that fuels the underlying infrastructure of polygon networks, facilitating the construction and interconnection of blockchain networks that operate on Ethereum technology.

It provides solutions to several of the predicaments encountered by Ethereum presently, including exorbitant fees, substandard user experience, and limited transactions per second, with the objective of establishing a diverse network of Ethereum-compliant blockchains.

At present, Ethereum stands as the second most prominent digital currency globally, as determined by its market capitalization, which represents the collective valuation of its circulating supply.

Presently, Polygon holds the fourteenth position among the most sizable cryptocurrencies globally, as determined by its market capitalization. Initially, the project was ushered in under the name of MATIC Network. Subsequently, it underwent a rebranding to "polygon" as its scope garnered increased public attention. The objective is to establish a unique blockchain infrastructure that facilitates the seamless transfer of both value and information.

The project pertains to some of the most prevalent domains within the realm of cryptocurrencies, including

DeFi (Decentralized Finance), DApp (Decentralized Application), DAO's (Decentralized Autonomous Organizations), and NFT's (Non-Fungible Tokens).

So Who Built Polygon?

Polygon is a network of Indian origin that has been constructed by a group of four software engineers, namely Jaynti Kanani, Sandeep Nailwal, Anurag Arjun, and Mihailo Bjelic.

Despite securing a position within the top 15 cryptocurrencies, the creators of Polygon possess grand aspirations to elevate it to the status of the third most prominent cryptographic undertaking, after Bitcoin and Ethereum.

The persistent ascent of Polygon (MATIC) can be attributed to various factors. It encompasses the escalating enthusiasm surrounding polygon, the announcement regarding Google BigQuery, and the investment made by Mark Cuban.

Around MATIC

Polygon's expansion can be attributed, in part, to the escalating prominence of the Ethereum network and the wide-scale embracing of its blockchain technology. The rapid and cost-effective transactions enabled by polygon's side chain infrastructure have generated a high level of excitement in terms of price and public perception.

On February 9, 2021, MATIC made a declaration of its intention to undergo a rebranding process, repositioning itself as a polygon with the aim of achieving international recognition. Polygon enhanced the system through the incorporation of promising metaverse initiatives and the integration of Matic Plasma Chain.

This infrastructure allowed Polygon to establish a layer one blockchain network equipped with integrated scaling solutions tailored to support NFT, DeFi, and other applications. In light of the escalating congestion and rising expenses on the Ethereum Network, there is a growing adoption and acceptance of Polygon's remarkably economical transaction fees. Due to a rising need for scalable networks, Polygon has the potential to incorporate additional projects.

The increasing uptake of polygon appears to enhance investors' general sentiment in the cryptocurrency market. Per LunarCrush's data, Polygon's presence across various social media platforms has experienced a notable surge of 636% over the preceding three-month period. This indicates that the investor has been displaying a heightened level of involvement in the currency that surpasses previous instances.

Cryptocurrencies Often Fail

Cryptocurrency start-ups are frequently regarded as highly lucrative investment prospects. Investors are strongly advised to strategically invest in the forthcoming Bitcoin opportunity at an early stage, as doing so may yield substantial financial gains in the subsequent week. The actuality is in stark contrast. Based on statistical data obtained from deadcoins.com, the number of failed cryptocurrencies surpasses 1,600 as of May 2021. These unsuccessful cryptocurrencies are categorized into respective groups titled as "deceased", "compromised", "frauds", or "satirical offerings." In this scenario, the term "failed" denotes that they exhibit markedly diminished trading volumes or have encountered a substantial decline in price from which they have not been able to rebound. When taking into account the fact that there exist approximately 4,000 cryptocurrencies as of May 2021, it presents a discouraging outlook for the long-term prospects of cryptocurrencies. Approximately 40% of all cryptocurrencies in existence thus far have experienced failure.

Numerous cryptocurrencies commence and conclude in a similar manner. Certain entities may initially generate significant hype but eventually succumb to insignificance as investors discern the absence of a functional or distinctive offering. Instances of failure occur when inadequate security measures open the door for malicious hackers to pilfer millions. Many individuals experience lack of success since they do not succeed in cultivating an online audience. The crucial aspect lies in the fact that the rise or fall of a cryptocurrency is not attributable to its inherent value, but rather hinges on its perception within the broader market.

Investing in a cryptocurrency start-up entails a level of risk akin to engaging in a game of chance, such as roulette, within a casino setting. You are placing your trust in the efficient online marketing of the cryptocurrency to attract individuals who believe they can also reap financial gains from it. Should the cryptocurrency fail to garner substantial attention and impetus, it will promptly take its place among the multitude of 1,600 unsuccessful cryptocurrencies.

Ponzi schemes involving crypto-based banking operations.

An additional Ponzi scheme that is relatively easy to detect within the realm of cryptocurrencies is observed in the emergence of online 'banks' centered around cryptocurrencies, which are frequently marketed as the future of a decentralized financial system. In a single instance, I did not need to disregard the initial page of their website before being alerted to concerning indicators. I shall refrain from disclosing the name of the company in this context; however, for the sake of clarity, I shall designate the said company as 'BrickFi'.

In the given instance, it is highlighted on their main page that they are promoting an impressive 8.6% interest rate for the cryptocurrency funds entrusted to their platform. Please be aware that presently, the majority of savings accounts offered by established financial institutions are yielding approximately 1% in interest. It is truly remarkable how reminiscent this appears, despite the fact that we find ourselves once more, presented in a monochromatic manner on their sophisticated web platform. Notwithstanding the initial indication of returns surpassing all other types of savings accounts by a significant margin, I proceeded to navigate to the lower section of their homepage in order to confirm whether my initial perception was inaccurate.

Continuing to browse through the homepage, I subsequently discovered that in addition to the opportunity to establish a savings account yielding a competitive interest rate of 8.6%, it was also possible to secure a loan with a minimum interest rate of 4.5%. It is evident to anyone with basic reasoning skills that the figures in question fail to converge. Examine any other financial institution across the globe and attempt to identify an establishment that surpasses the level of interest paid on their savings accounts, derived from the loans they extend. I will simplify the process for you; you will not be able to locate one.

The underlying reason for this is that a bank's functioning primarily revolves around providing interest payments on the funds that investors have entrusted with the bank. In the current year of 2021, it would be advantageous for an individual seeking to save money to attain a 1% interest rate on their savings by engaging with a conventional financial institution as an illustration. From where does the bank derive the funds necessary to remunerate these investors with their respective interest? The bank utilizes the funds originally deposited by lending them to individuals, who subsequently pay interest on the borrowed amount. In the year 2021, individuals seeking financial assistance may secure a personal loan from a reputable banking institution and anticipate a favorable interest rate of 2.9%. Therefore, the bank achieves a net gain of 2.9% after deducting the 1% payout, resulting in a profit of 1.9%. That is an overly simplistic depiction of the operational mechanics behind traditional banking institutions.

Presently, consider this captivating novel digital currency institution offering a remarkable 8.6% interest rate on deposited funds, while exclusively imposing a mere 4.5% interest rate on extended loans. This implies that they are experiencing an average decline of 4.1%. Once more, it is evident that even without the wisdom of Warren Buffet, it is clear that the financial statements of this company will not be reconcilable.

This company exhibits numerous indicators that align with the red flags highlighted by the Securities and Exchange Commission in identifying potential Ponzi schemes. From the outset, they make assurances of exceptional returns for a savings account with minimal risk. This presents an initial indication of concern. Another cause for concern is that these returns are purportedly guaranteed to yield a steady 8.6%.

The third matter pertains to a convergence of three indicators of concern identified by the SEC. These issues pertain to their documentation, the lack of registration as sellers, and the absence of registration for their investments. Indeed, despite initial appearances, they are not actually registered as an investment company. Although they maintain registration with the Securities and Exchange

Commission as a "pooled investment fund," a cursory Google search and a brief review of their SEC filing reveal that they have not obtained registration as an investment company, as mandated by the Investment Company Act of 1940. This implies that they are granted exemption from a significant amount of regulatory scrutiny. The disclosure regarding the lack of financial protections from regulatory bodies and the possibility of total loss of principal is only found when extensively examining the fine print on their website.

The fourth indication of concern pertains to the potential challenges that a user may encounter in the process of withdrawing payments. When a user initiates a withdrawal request, it may require a maximum of seven days for the withdrawal to be processed. It is asserted that "This provides an opportunity to retrieve loans, if necessary." Furthermore, this demonstrates a characteristic commonly associated with Ponzi schemes.

Lastly, the ultimate cause for concern lies in the methodology they purport to employ in order to generate these returns for potential investors. Their elucidation regarding the manner in which they generate such formidable returns lacks specificity and fails to furnish any comprehensive information. The provided explanations also lack comprehensive elucidation of the associated risks. Once again, the remarkable parallels between this scheme and other Ponzi schemes are readily apparent.

One disconcerting aspect of enterprises of this nature extends beyond the obvious risk they pose to investors who entrust their finances in hopes of substantial returns. Moreover, these firms offer loans whereby they secure collateral twice the value of the loan. Additionally, it should be noted that they function as a cryptocurrency exchange. This implies that the potential for schemes of this nature to defraud individuals is significant. They will possess the capability to exploit three diverse customer categories, encompassing more than just individuals seeking to save. The Ponzi scheme is unarguably undergoing significant transformations to adapt to the demands of the modern era. Despite the glaringly evident indicators of fraudulent activities, these enterprises persist in thriving and proliferating.

The Prevalent Currencies In The Global Foreign Exchange Market

In essence, engaging in FOREX trading entails the diligent manipulation of the global reserve of currencies. There exist certain currencies that hold a prominent position in the global currency domain, namely the US Dollar, the British Pound Sterling, the Japanese Yen, the Euro, and the Swiss Franc. Additionally, notable currencies include the Canadian and Australian Dollar, Chinese Yuan, and Mexican Peso.

Each of these currencies is traded freely within the FOREX market, allowing individuals to engage in buying and selling transactions based on prevailing market rates and the existing supply of these currencies. As a result, you possess ample prospects to maximize your profitability, leveraging the trades you execute.

Ultimately, the attainment of financial gain relies on comprehending the intricacies of diverse currencies and their interplay. This is predominantly contingent upon the interrelationships between nations and the frequency at which these currencies are exchanged in tandem. Furthermore, it should be noted that there are currencies that are typically not exchanged in conjunction with one another. In such instances, one must employ a greater degree of ingenuity. However, it is possible to engage in currency trading at any given moment. It is your responsibility to conduct thorough research on the optimal combinations that align with your specific investment strategy.

As an illustration, in the event that you opt for a cautious approach, adhering to widely-recognized currencies would be the most secure course of action. If you possess a strong desire to achieve potentially substantial profits, you may want to consider venturing down an unconventional path. This infers engaging in the exchange of currencies that may not necessarily be frequently paired. The ultimate determinant lies in the primary goal that you have envisioned.

Nevertheless, it is important to note that for inexperienced investors, it is advisable to adhere to more widely traded currency pairings. As you accumulate further expertise, you can explore opportunities with different currencies. It is crucial to refrain from undertaking avoidable risks at this juncture in the game.

Major Currency Pairings

In the realm of the foreign exchange market, it is evident that specific currency pairs exercise a considerable influence over the dynamics of trading. These pairs are commonly referred to as "correlated pairs" due to their frequent trading activity. Hence, sufficient evidence exists to indicate that their movements align with the price action of one another. When a substantial fluctuation occurs in one currency, it exerts a direct influence on the counterpart. Gaining an understanding of the inherent characteristics of these pairings will facilitate the attainment of reliable profitability. While they might not be exceptionally impressive, they will undoubtedly provide sufficient illumination.

The following are the primary currency pairs that are currently traded in the FOREX market:

- The EUR/USD pairing is widely regarded as the most frequently traded duo within the foreign exchange

(FOREX) market. It comprises approximately 20% of the total volume of transactions. For those who are new to investing, this represents the most secure option to initiate their journey. Within this platform, you can discover reliable outcomes that will facilitate your financial gains without delay. You also have the option to replicate trades. That renders the initiation process even more convenient.

- The USD/JPY is commonly recognized as the second most actively traded currency pair. Nevertheless, the USD/EUR pair dominates trading volume to a significantly greater extent.

- The GBP/USD is additionally considered to be the third-ranked pair. • The GBP/USD is also recognized as the pair ranking third. • The GBP/USD is likewise deemed to be the pair occupying the third position. This currency pair is predominantly traded within the European segment of the market. The Euro is the favored choice among the majority of American investors.

The USD/CHF pair is frequently traded, although its market share is significantly lower compared to other currency pairs.

• Additional noteworthy pairs encompass the USD/CAD, AUD/USD, and the NZD/USD. The NZD/AUD pair is similarly correlated, but its market share is not as substantial as that of other pairs mentioned in this list.

It is prudent to adhere to the major currency pairs while initially venturing into the realm of the FOREX market. As previously stated, with the accumulation of experience in the market, one's capacity for creativity becomes more pronounced. Indeed, that assertion holds true, as unconventional combinations often present opportunities for substantial profits.

Nevertheless, it is advisable to thoroughly examine these pairs prior to making a commitment. Although there is a high likelihood of achieving success, there is also a substantial possibility of falling short. Consequently, ensure that you thoroughly complete your assignments prior to embarking on this venture.

Assessing the Valuation of Key Currency Pairings

We highly advise inexperienced investors to engage in trading major currency pairs primarily due to the significant trading volume involved. These currencies possess the highest volume of transactional activity. Consequently, inexperienced investors can anticipate a higher return on investment, figuratively speaking.

When there is a higher magnitude of trading volume, the likelihood of the effectiveness of the strategies we have elucidated in this book increases. In situations where the trading volume is reduced, the efficacy of the strategies outlined in this document may be somewhat compromised. Therefore, it is imperative to ensure stringent oversight when transacting with obscure currencies.

With that being stated, the value of major currency pairs is determined by the interplay between supply and demand. Hence, a substantial increase in trading volume has the effect of mitigating substantial fluctuations in the price of prominent currency pairs. Conversely, currencies with limited trading volume can experience substantial fluctuations as a result of a solitary trade. This has the potential to adversely impact your ability to generate a financial gain.

When dealing with considerable institutional investors, particularly those with multimillion-dollar positions, they typically gravitate towards major currencies as opposed to lesser-known ones, primarily due to the abundant supply that can accommodate such substantial trading positions. Therefore, smaller investors have the opportunity to benefit from the success of larger investors. By engaging in trading activities alongside large corporations, one has the opportunity to capitalize on market surges. While this may not result in generating millions of dollars, it undeniably serves as an excellent means of earning a substantial profit.

As an illustration, the exchange rate between the Euro and the United States Dollar is currently recorded as 1.10. This implies that the value of one Euro is equivalent to $1.10. In the event that the price undergoes a sudden change to 1.12, it indicates that the Euro has appreciated in relation to the dollar, resulting in an increase in the amount of dollars required to acquire a Euro. Nevertheless, should the price decrease to $1.08, it can be observed that the dollar has appreciated in value, since it requires a lesser quantity of dollars to acquire a single Euro. Based on your strategic choices, you can emerge as the victor. It is essential to remember that the behavior of price action among the major currency pairs will be ultimately influenced by the various factors present in the market. Consequently, maintain constant vigilance.

Investing in Cryptocurrency

In recent times, there has been a notable surge in the popularity of cryptocurrencies, commonly referred to as cryptos, particularly in light of the exponential growth of Bitcoin. The dramatic ascent of Bitcoin to a value exceeding $20,000 per coin drew widespread attention to cryptocurrencies. Due to the significant potential benefits of cryptocurrencies, virtually anyone who had the opportunity to enter the crypto market chose to do so. Regrettably, a portion of individuals suffered significant losses as the price of Bitcoin plummeted. However, Bitcoin does not reign supreme as the sole contender in this arena.

However, cryptocurrencies remain relatively unfamiliar to the typical investor. Hence, we shall proceed to discuss the nature of cryptocurrencies and the potential for generating profits through crypto trading. Moreover, it can be observed that cryptocurrencies are still in the early stages of development. This indicates a significant advantageous potential that can be leveraged.

It is crucial to emphasize the reality that cryptocurrencies do not constitute conventional currency. A cryptocurrency denotes a form of digital currency that serves the purpose of facilitating transaction settlements and fulfilling various other purposes. As an example, if one party were to sell a vehicle to another, the transaction could be concluded through the exchange of digital tokens rather than the utilization of conventional currency. This is the aspect that renders cryptocurrencies highly captivating for the typical investor.

When engaging in cryptocurrency transactions, one is effectively engaging in transactions involving binary code, specifically the representation of data through the digits 1 and 0. These can serve for purposes of identification, monitoring quantity, and even aiding governmental initiatives. Certainly, cryptos have a multitude of applications.

Currently, the valuation of cryptocurrencies is observed in conventional currencies like the United States Dollar. In this particular scenario, the acquisition of cryptocurrencies can be facilitated through the exchange of US Dollars (or any other officially recognized currency). The digital tokens are securely stored within a virtual wallet or vault. This secure repository holds the codes that grant access to your cryptocurrency holdings. Subsequently, you have the option to engage in the barter of these tokens with fellow users, receiving in return either alternative tokens or conventional forms of currency.

It is important to highlight that cryptocurrencies do not exhibit the trading patterns observed in traditional currency exchanges such as the FOREX market. They exhibit characteristics akin to commodities in terms of their trading patterns. Oil serves as a suitable reference point for assessing the comparative worth of cryptocurrencies. Crude oil is classified as a tradable commodity, with its market value determined by spot pricing. Spot price refers to the prevailing price of the commodity at the moment the trade is executed. Therefore, identical market forces are applicable in this context. The valuation of all cryptocurrencies is determined by the interplay of supply and demand. Certain individuals possess a substantial distribution, exemplified by a vast quantity of coins numbering in the millions. Contingent upon their level of popularity, investors may opt to allocate a progressively elevated valuation towards these assets.

Trading Cryptocurrencies

Cryptocurrencies are not traded within the public market. Consequently, it is imperative that you undergo a cryptocurrency exchange. The mechanics of these exchanges operate in a similar fashion to that of the foreign exchange market (FOREX). The distinction exists in the fact that you are not engaging in the exchange of "genuine" currencies. Instead, you are solely engaged in handling cryptocurrencies.

Within a cryptocurrency exchange, it is possible to acquire digital coins using traditional currencies such as the US Dollar. Subsequently, you may proceed to vend them to fellow users at a gain or loss, contingent upon the result of the transaction. In lieu of that, you may opt to retain them for an extended duration of your preference. It is crucial to be aware of the cost factor.

Due to the unrestricted volatility of prices, it is essential to closely monitor the quotations pertaining to established cryptocurrencies. Hence, it is possible for you to monitor their worth and proceed with the sale at your discretion. It is important to mention that cryptocurrency trading is significantly less complex in comparison to foreign exchange trading. A complex setup is not necessary for cryptocurrency trading. All that is required is to engage in the process of purchasing and subsequently selling. Nevertheless, it is imperative to remain focused on the task at hand.

A notable advantage lies in the relatively lower trading volume of cryptocurrencies compared to that of the foreign exchange market. Therefore, it would be unreasonable to anticipate precise price fluctuations on a second-by-second basis. One can ascertain the price movement across significantly longer durations, spanning hours or even days. If one possesses a high level of competence in the interpretation of charts, it becomes quite effortless to discern recurring patterns within them. Consequently, you will be spared the arduous task of poring over extensive technical information for hours.

Optimal Cryptocurrencies for Trading" "Top-Ranked Cryptocurrencies for Trading" "Superior Cryptocurrencies for Trading" "Most Favorable Cryptocurrencies for Trading

This is a question that is commonly posed. For the majority of individuals, cryptocurrencies are synonymous with Bitcoin. As we have previously stipulated, Bitcoin does not monopolize the landscape.

Presented below are the 10 most significant cryptocurrencies available for trading today, classified according to their respective market capitalizations:

- Cryptocurrency known as Bitcoin

- The cryptocurrency known as Ethereum • The digital currency by the name of Ethereum • The virtual currency referred to as Ethereum • The online monetary system known as

Ethereum • The blockchain-based currency commonly known as Ethereum

• The digital asset known as XRP

• Securely fasten • Attach firmly • Tightly connect • Affix securely • Fix tightly • Fasten securely

• Bitcoin Cash

• Bitcoin Satoshi Vision

• The digital currency known as Litecoin

• End of Sentence

• BNB (Binance Coin) • The digital asset known as Binance Coin (BNB) • BNB (Binance Coin) token

• The cryptocurrency known as Tezos

Although this list is not comprehensive (given the presence of over 5,000 cryptocurrencies in the current market), these options present the most promising opportunity for generating profitable returns through trading. You may explore a cryptocurrency exchange platform such as Coinbase in order to acquire further information on the process of account opening. Subsequently, you may commence engaging in the trading of these digital currencies. One advantage of this compilation is that each item is priced differently. Therefore, there is no need for you to expend $10,000 to acquire a single Bitcoin. In reality, certain trades occur at a mere fraction of the Dollar's value. Consequently, there is a cost that suits every individual.

While it is true that alternative exchanges exist, it is important to note that equivalent regulations govern them as well. It is crucial to prioritize renowned companies that possess a strong reputation and a proven history of success. Furthermore, it should be noted that trusted cryptocurrency trading platforms provide extensive assistance to their users. Indeed, their core interest lies in optimizing trade facilitation with the ultimate goal of inclusivity, enabling the participation of others. As a result, one can anticipate receiving substantial assistance when initiating crypto trading endeavors.

www.ingramcontent.com/pod-product-compliance
Lightning Source LLC
Chambersburg PA
CBHW050239120526
44590CB00016B/2155